YR 1998

AF470052

Coastline Journey

Contents

Introduction

The British Isles is a group of islands, surrounded by four seas. The countries of England, Wales and Scotland are on the largest island. Northern Ireland is part of the second largest island. Nowhere in Britain is more than 121 kilometres from the sea.

The islands are made of different kinds of rocks. There are older, harder rocks which were made between 3000 million and 345 million years ago. The newer, softer rocks were made between 345 million and 25 million years ago. The youngest rocks in Britain are only two million years old! They are in East Anglia.

The east and west coasts

The west side of Britain is mostly made of old rocks. The coastline has many high, rocky cliffs. The rocks are hard so the sea cannot wear them away easily.

Parts of the eastern side of Britain are made up of newer rocks. These are being worn away by the sea. Every year metres of this eastern coast disappear into the sea. Flat parts of the east coast are also in danger from sea floods.

Rocky cliffs at Land's End, Cornwall

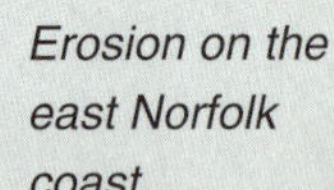
Erosion on the east Norfolk coast.

Orkney Islands
Shetland
North Sea
Outer Hebrides
SCOTLAND
Atlantic Ocean
5
THE JOURNEY
1 The journey starts in the most crowded area, the south-east . . .
2 then to the south-west corner . . .
3 around the coast of Wales . . .
4 up through the north-west of England and over to Northern Ireland . . .
5 along to the north edge of Scotland . . .
6 and down the north-east coast of England.
6
NORTHERN IRELAND
4
IRELAND
Irish Sea
1
WALES
ENGLAND
3
2
Isles of Scilly
English Channel
Channel Islands
3

The journey begins

The journey begins along the low, sandy coast of East Anglia. This stretches north from London. Some parts of East Anglia are lost every year because its soft, sandy cliffs crumble into the sea.

The coast of East Anglia is quiet. The coast south of London is much busier.

Tourism is a big industry for most places along the coast. Every year, thousands of tourists visit the holiday towns of Great Yarmouth, Margate and Brighton.

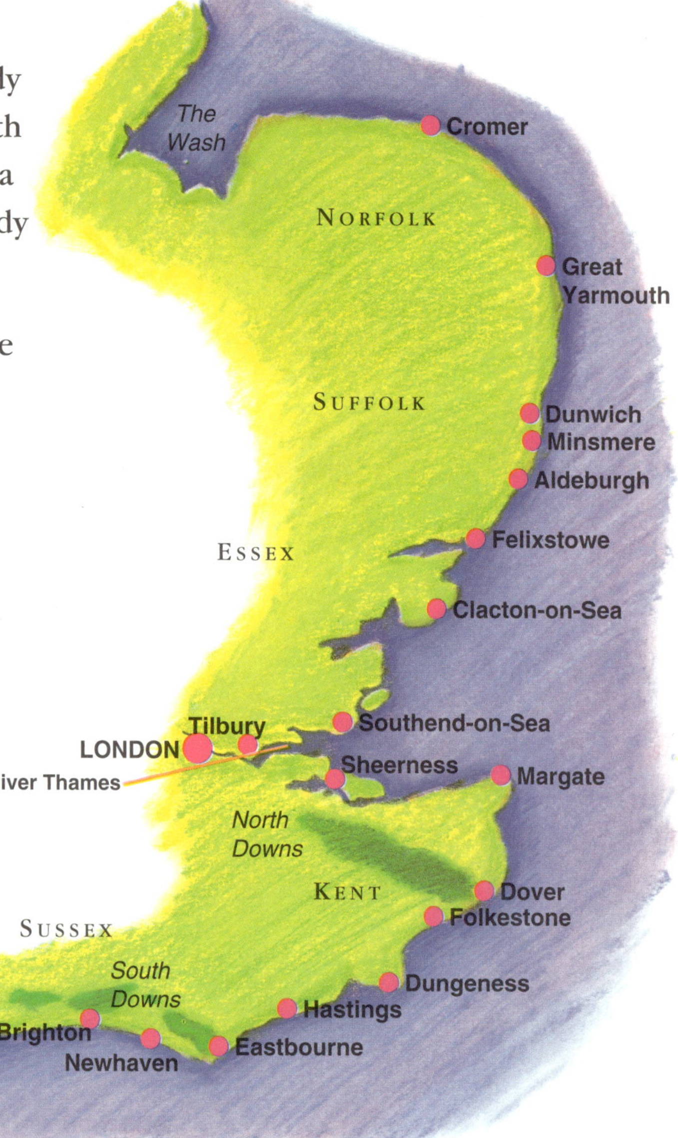

Brighton Beach is crowded with tourists in the summer.

There is a colony of common seals in Norfolk. It is the largest colony of common seals in Britain.

 ## *Where people work*

Many people work on the Channel ferries and in the busy ferry ports. These ports are open 24 hours a day. Felixstowe, Tilbury and Sheerness are ports too, but they are for container ships. These ships carry cargoes such as timber and grain.

The busiest sea lanes in the world are off the Coast of Dover. All kinds of ships sail there, from huge oil tankers to small sailing boats.

Tilbury

Dover Castle

This part of Britain has always been in danger of invasions. Castles and forts were built all round the coast to defend it. When the Romans invaded Britain, they made Dover the headquarters of their navy. Inside Dover castle are the remains of a Roman lighthouse.

Felixstowe

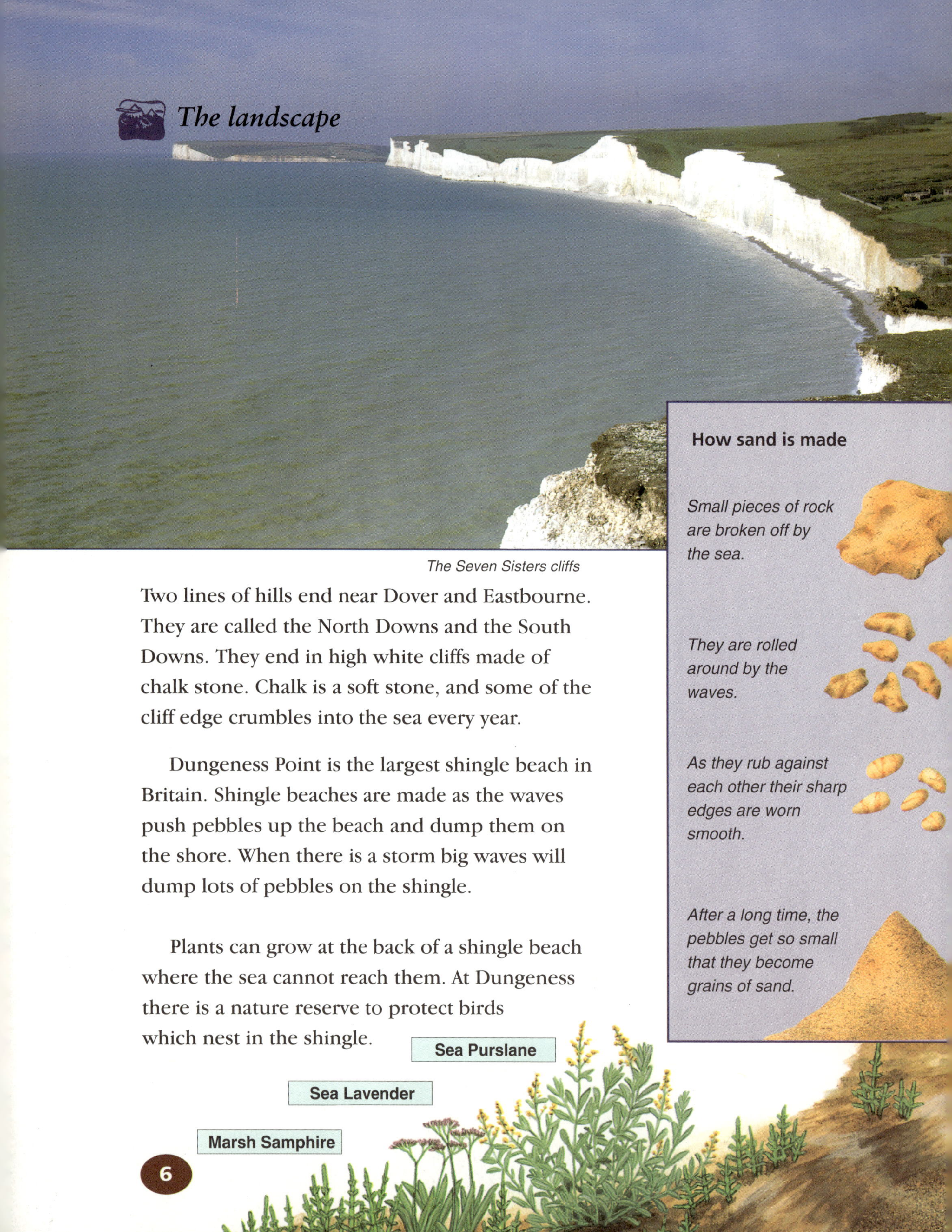

The Seven Sisters cliffs

Two lines of hills end near Dover and Eastbourne. They are called the North Downs and the South Downs. They end in high white cliffs made of chalk stone. Chalk is a soft stone, and some of the cliff edge crumbles into the sea every year.

Dungeness Point is the largest shingle beach in Britain. Shingle beaches are made as the waves push pebbles up the beach and dump them on the shore. When there is a storm big waves will dump lots of pebbles on the shingle.

Plants can grow at the back of a shingle beach where the sea cannot reach them. At Dungeness there is a nature reserve to protect birds which nest in the shingle.

The wildlife

Norfolk has some of the largest salt marshes in Europe. A salt marsh is made when plants grow in the mud where a river flows into the sea.

All the land around The Wash used to be salt marshes. The sea water was drained from some of the salt marshes so the land could be farmed.

The plants found growing on the salt marshes do not mind being covered by the sea when the tide comes in. Birds come to the salt marshes to feed on the creatures that live in the mud.

Travelling west

This part of the coast is shaped like a foot. The toe points west towards America. A piece of land shaped like this and surrounded on three sides by the sea is called a peninsula. At the end of the south-west peninsula, the English Channel becomes the Atlantic Ocean.

These are the ruins of Tintagel Castle. Local legend says that King Arthur was born here.

Surfing is popular along this coast.

Where people work

Tourism is the most important industry in the south-west. People come from all over Britain and Europe to surf, sail and swim. Many of them stay in the small fishing villages which get very crowded in the summer.

Many jobs in this area are to do with the sea and ships. Ships are built in Appledore. Warships and submarines are repaired in Plymouth. Near Plymouth there is a school that trains deep-sea divers. Some of these divers will go to work on oil rigs.

The Royal Navy's air-sea rescue station is at Culdrose, on the Lizard. It is the biggest helicopter base in Europe, with 3000 people and 80 helicopters. In 1993 they flew 200 rescue missions, and saved 124 lives.

Saving lives by helicopter

Sandstone cliffs

 ## *The landscape*

This stretch of coast is very rocky. The earth and rocks around Torquay are made of bright red sandstone. The waves have worn the coast away into arches and caves. Further down, the cliffs are made of harder stone, called granite. The Atlantic waves have broken off granite boulders.

Granite cliffs

Cornwall's past

Long ago, some people would trick ships on to the rocky coast in the dark. These people were called wreckers. The wreckers would shine lights on the shore. The lights looked like house and harbour lights. When the ship had crashed on the rocks the wreckers would steal the cargo.

The hundreds of caves and hidden coves also made good landing places for smugglers. They smuggled in alcohol and tobacco.

There are metals in the rocks, and copper and tin were mined here. Most of the mines shut down nearly a hundred years ago. Now all that is left of them are ruined buildings standing on the cliffs.

An English smuggler

The wildlife

Red Valerian and bright yellow gorse are easy to find on the cliff tops. Other plants grow on ledges down the face of the cliff.

When the tide goes out it leaves water between rocks on the shore. Rock pools are home to small crabs, sea anemones and shellfish like limpets and winkles.

At Navax Point, near St Ives', the sea has worn deep caves. People cannot reach the caves by land. Grey seals can breed here, safe from humans.

Crossing the Severn

To get to Wales by road from the south-west of England you must cross Britain's longest river, the Severn. Where a river flows into the sea is called an estuary. The Severn estuary is over 48 kilometres long. It has one of the highest tides in the world. Specially high tides bring a three-metre tidal wave surging up the river. The tidal wave is called a bore. Surfers can ride the Severn Bore inland for 80 kilometres.

The Severn
Bridge

 ## *Where people work*

Milford Haven is one of Britain's largest oil tanker harbours. The water is deep enough for huge tankers.

Fishing takes place all round the Welsh coast, but the boats are small, in-shore boats, not big, deep-sea trawlers. They catch sea-bass, plaice and the salmon that swim up from the Atlantic into the rivers.

Milford Haven

The railway by the sea

Slate was quarried from huge caverns in the mountains at Blainau Ffestiniog a hundred years ago. Many buildings have roofs made of Welsh slate. The quarries are closed now. The railway that used to take the slates down to ships now carries tourists up to visit the caverns.

Slate cavern at Blainau Ffestiniog

The landscape

Much of the Welsh coast is long sandy beaches. Many tourists come on holiday here, to the beautiful beaches on the Gower Peninsula.

This coast also has a history of mining. Slate was quarried on the west coast. Coal was mined on the south coast. The Romans came to Britain because they heard of the silver and gold in the Welsh mountains. Gold can still be found washed down in the sands of the estuary near Barmouth. Royal wedding rings are always made of Welsh gold.

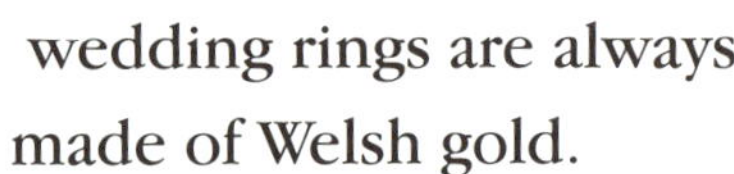

Rhossili Bay on the Gower Peninsula.

How sand dunes build up

When strong winds blow on to a sandy beach, the sand is piled up into dunes. These can be 30 metres high. The wind moves the dunes inland. If the dunes are not stopped they can cover buildings and farmland. At Kenfig, a whole town was buried under the dunes in the Middle Ages.

The dunes are planted with marram grass to stop them moving. This is a tough grass with roots which hold the sand in place.

The wildlife

Sand does not hold rain water. This makes sand dunes very dry places for plants to grow. Many dune plants have leaves that trap or store water.

The dips in between the dunes are called dune slacks. Slacks are wetter places, and unusual plants grow in the damp soil.

The rare Natterjack Toad lives in damp dune slacks. There are very few places left in Britain where this toad can breed.

Other animals and insects live among the dunes. Some of them may leave tracks in the sand.

Travelling north

The Blackpool illuminations

Carrick-a-rede is a limestone headland on the coast of Northern Ireland. Each spring, a rope bridge is put up across the inlet. Local salmon fishermen put it up to give them a path across the gorge.

The journey continues up the north-west coast of England, visiting coast of Northern Ireland. Many sea-side towns around the Irish Sea grew up as holiday towns.

Blackpool is one of Britain's biggest resorts. It has a sea front 11 kilometres long. Ten million visitors a year go to see the famous lights that decorate the sea front.

There is not much activity along the rest of the coast up to where Scotland begins. Most tourists go inland to the Lake District.

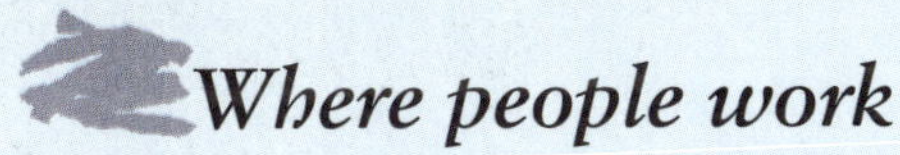
Where people work

There is a reservoir of gas 100 metres below the Irish Sea. It is 18 kilometres square, and it is 42 kilometres west of Blackpool. Five drilling platforms stand over it. They are connected to a central processing platform. 300 people work on the platform, including engineers, radio operators, cooks and medical staff. Every day boats and helicopters come out from the mainland with crew and supplies.

The gas is piped to land through 37 kilometres of pipe buried one metre under the sea bed. Barrow, on the mainland, has a processing plant for sea gas. Gas from under the Irish Sea is piped to the plant. The plant prepares it for being piped to houses. A smell has to be added to sea gas so that people will know if there is a gas leak.

Barrow processing platform

 # *The landscape*

Most of this coast is sandy, with long stretches of dunes.
There are sandstone cliffs at St Bees Head and at
Whitehaven there is coal in the ground. The Isle of Man,
off the coast, has mountains in the centre made of slate.

The Giant's Causeway

Northern Ireland has one of
the most famous rock
formations in Britain. The
Giant's Causeway is made of
blocks of basalt, a hard, black
rock. Liquid basalt poured out
of a volcano millions of years
ago. As it cooled, it hardened
into these six-sided columns.

The wildlife

Rivers from the Lake District flow into the Irish Sea. Their wide estuaries are important feeding places for birds.

Morecambe Bay is about 16 kilometres wide. Three rivers run into it. Quicksands and fast tides make the bay dangerous for people to walk on. Special guides called 'Queen's Guides to the Sands' lead walkers across at low tide.

Standing on the sands is easy, however, for long-legged wading birds. They use their long beaks to find worms and shellfish under the mud.

Other birds nest in the reeds and marshes around the estuary. Flounder, plaice, whitebait and shrimps live in the waters of Morecambe Bay.

All six kinds of British amphibians live around the Ravenglass estuary. These include the rare Natterjack Toad and the Great Crested Newt, which looks like a tiny dinosaur.

The wild coast

The north coast of Scotland is the wildest part of the Scottish coast. The Dunnet Head lighthouse stands on the most northern part of the British mainland. The cliffs there are battered by fierce North Atlantic gales. The sea off Dunnet Head is called the Pentland Firth. It is one of the most dangerous stretches of water on earth.

Fewer people live here than in any other part of Britain. There are not many fishing villages along the coast. The weather makes it difficult for fishermen to make a living. At the Butt of Lewis in the Outer Hebrides there is a gale one day in every six.

Dunnet Head lighthouse

Where people work

Many tourists visit the islands off Scotland's coast, to enjoy the peace and quiet.

They buy the tweed and knitted goods that are traditional in this area. This is the home of the Shetland jumper and of knitted shawls as fine as cobwebs.

Small farmers called crofters live in lonely cottages along the coast. Crofters keep a few animals, catch fish and grow crops (like oats) for their families to eat.

Other people work in the new industries such as the nuclear plant at Dounreay. Many also work for the oil industry of the North Sea. They work on the oil rigs, or help to load tankers with oil.

Weaving on a traditional loom.

A hat made from tweed.

A crofter's cottage

Lifeboat rescues

The lifeboats of this coast are called "all-weather lifeboats". They must be prepared to go out in storms and rough seas. In 1993 they were launched 93 times, and saved 53 lives.

The Old Man of Hoy

The landscape

The mountains and cliffs are made of hard types of rock called granite and gneiss. Gneiss is the oldest rock in Britain. The Orkneys and the land behind Dunnet Head are made of the same red sandstone that is in the south-west of England.

The sea wears the soft sandstone into strange shapes. The Old Man of Hoy, in Orkney, is a famous pillar of rock. Pillars like this are called stacks. They are left after the sea has worn the land that joined them to the main cliff.

Kidney vetch   Spearwort   Selfheal

The wildlife

The people who lived on this coast in the past were often a long way from doctors. They used many plants as medicines: Kidney vetch was used for cuts and bruises; Spearwort was used to stop pain; Selfheal was used for illnesses of the liver.

The island of animals

St Kilda is a group of wild islands which have the highest cliffs in Europe. These are home to puffins, gannets and fulmars. The last people to live in St. Kilda left sixty years ago. They left behind their Soay sheep, the only wild British sheep. Soay sheep will not live together in herds, and they graze on the beaches, eating seaweed. The St Kilda wren and the St Kilda field mouse are two other animals only found here. St Kilda is the only part of Britain that is a world heritage site.

The journey ends

The coastline in the north-east of England has two very different parts. Just down from Scotland, lonely sandy beaches and lines of sand dunes stretch for miles. At Bamburgh and Dunstanburgh, castles stand by the shore. There are other small fishing villages but most of this coastline is deserted.

Things change at the estuaries of the two great rivers, the Tyne and the Tees. This is one of the most industrial parts of Britain.

Lindisfarne

The island of Lindisfarne is linked to the coast by a flat road. The tide sweeps in to cover this road twice a day, cutting off the island for hours.

Kippers being dried

Where people work

Fishing is an important industry. Boats go out from the villages for shellfish such as crabs, scallops and mussels. The village of Craster is famous for its kippers. These are Scottish herrings, dried by being hung over smoky fires.

Coal-mining and ship-building used to be important industries in this area. Now there is not much ship-building, and coal mines are being closed. The end of this work means that many people in this region are unemployed.

A fishing boat

The life boat heroine

Grace Darling was the daughter of the lighthouse keeper on the Farne Islands. On September 7th 1838 the steamship 'Forfarshire' hit a rock on the Farnes in a fierce storm. The weather was too rough for the lifeboat to leave the shore. Grace and her father rowed their boat through mountainous seas for about two kilometres to rescue nine people. She was given a Gold Medal for her bravery.

The landscape

The quiet part of the coast is limestone and sandstone. This makes good farming soil, long beaches and lines of dunes. The coal is mined from the surface of the ground on the coast around Newcastle. Coal mines go out for almost seven kilometres under the sea, and lumps of sea coal can be picked up off the beaches.

Coal

How coal is formed

Trees and plants die and fall on the ground.

They form a layer of rotting vegetation

After thousands of years, a layer of coal is formed.

How a limestone fossil is formed

Limestone is made from the crushed shells of tiny sea creatures that lived millions of years ago. As they died, their shells sank to the floor, mixed with mud and hardened.

A sea creature that lived millions of years ago.

The sea creature dies.

The dead sea creature's shell sinks into the mud.

After millions of years it hardens and becomes a fossil.

26

Limestone fossil

The wildlife

The Farne Islands are not much more than rocks sticking up out of the North Sea. Many sea birds nest on the rocks, where their eggs and chicks are safe from humans and animals who might harm them. Thousands of other sea birds visit the Farne Islands.

The most famous Farne Island bird is the Eider Duck. It is one of the world's commonest sea ducks. Long ago St Cuthbert lived on the rocky island. He stopped people killing the ducks to eat them. Since then the ducks have been known locally as Cuddy's ducks.

The Grey Seal had almost died out early in the 20th century. Now half the world's Grey Seals breed around Britain's coast. The largest English colony of Grey Seals breed on the Farne Islands.

An A to Z of animals and plants

Not all the changes that have been happening around the British coast are good for the countryside. Pollution by industry is damaging the sea and the animals that live in it. Every year, more tourists want to visit the coast, and more deserted land is used for roads and buildings. There is good news too, however. Animals, birds and plants are protected by nature reserves all round the coast. Some parts of the underwater 'countryside' around the coast are being protected as marine reserves.

Here are some plants and animals to look out for.

Basking Shark
Looks dangerous, but is harmless. It eats only plankton and likes the unpolluted waters off the western Scottish coast. It is threatened by pollution and by hunters, who kill it for its oil.

Bird's Foot Trefoil
A plant that grows on grassy clifftops. It is sometimes called 'eggs and bacon' because of the two colours of the flowers.

Common Blue Butterfly
This butterfly's caterpillars eat Bird's Foot Trefoil, which grows round the coasts.

Common Seal

A smaller and less common seal that the Grey Seal. It breeds on quiet sandbanks, particularly around The Wash.

Gannet

The largest white British sea bird. It nests on rocky shores and islands around our northern coasts. Catches fish by folding its wings and diving into the water at 97 kilometres per hour.

Common Spotted Orchid

A plant that needs to grow in undisturbed grassland. So many of Britain's fields are farmed that the Spotted Orchid has had to find a home on the coast. It grows along quiet grassy cliffs in a few places.

Glasswort

(also called Samphire)
This plant looks a bit like a cactus. It grows on salt marshes. On the East Anglian and North Sea coasts it is picked and eaten. It can either be boiled or pickled.

Cormorant

A large dark sea bird which nests all round the British coasts. Catches fish by swimming and diving from the surface of the water.

Grey Seal

This had almost been wiped out by hunters a hundred years ago. It is now a protected animal and its numbers are increasing, though it is thought to be damaged by North Sea pollution.

Cuckoo Wrasse

A brightly coloured fish that is found all round Britain's rocky coast but especially in the West of Britain.

Herring Gull

The most common large British gull, found all round the coast. Nests on all kinds of coast, and in winter it also comes inland to feed.

Horned Poppy

A bright flower that grows on shingle and sand dunes all round Britain, except in northern Scotland. Its big yellow flowers are very pretty, but all parts of the plant are poisonous and it is dangerous to pick it.

Natterjack Toad

A lot of the heathland the Natterjack toad lives on has been used for building, so this is now a rare toad. It breeds in warm pools behind sand dunes. It is now protected by nature reserves.

Icelandic pony

A tough little pony found on the islands off the coast of Scotland, where it can live partly on seaweed. Its ancestors were prehistoric European animals.

Otters

Numbers have dropped in England, due to hunting and pollution of their food and river homes by pesticides. There has also been human disturbance of the quiet riverbanks the otters need. The quiet coasts of northern Scotland are safe for otters who live on fish and shellfish.

Lundy Cabbage

One of the few plants that belong only to Britain. It is only found in one place, on the cliffs of the rocky island of Lundy, in the Bristol Channel.

Puffin

Lives at sea all winter. Comes inland to breed in summer, when its clown-markings are brighter. Nests in burrows in sandy turf. The numbers of puffins around Britain are dropping. This may be because of pollution, or fishermen taking too many sand-eels, which puffins need for food.

Marram Grass

This tough grass is called a 'dune builder' because its roots hold the sand grains and slowly build the level of the dune higher. If sand buries it, it can grow out again very fast. It has stiff leaves which can prick and scratch.

Purple Laver

A common seaweed found all round the coast. Like many seaweeds, it is full of vitamins. In South Wales people make 'laverbread' for breakfast by frying purple laver with oatmeal.

Six-spot Burnet Moth

This moth's caterpillars also eat Bird's Foot Trefoil growing around cliffs and dunes. The moth's bright colours warn birds not to eat it.

Sea-aster

A pale purple flower that grows on sea-marshes and cliffs and all round the British coasts. It can also grow in polluted river estuaries. The Elizabethans grew it in their gardens.

Thrift (also called Sea Pink)

A small plant that grows on cliffs and sea-marshes all round the coast and on mountain-tops in Britain. It is called thrift because it 'thrives' (grows well) in rocky places with very little soil.

Sea-buckthorn

Grows naturally along the east coast. Its roots hold sandy soil together, so it is planted along sandy coasts around Britain to stop erosion.

Sea-campion

A plant with a balloon-like tube under each white flower. It grows on cliffs and in shingle all round Britain.

Index